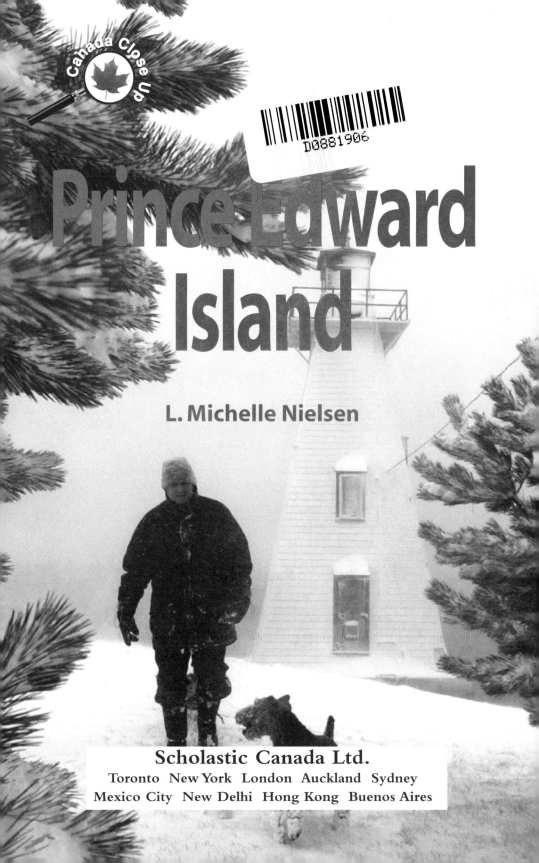

Canada Close Up

Prince Edward Island

Island

L. Michelle Nielsen

Scholastic Canada Ltd.
Toronto New York London Auckland Sydney
Mexico City New Delhi Hong Kong Buenos Aires

Visual Credits

Cover: Barrett & Mackay ©AllCanadaPhotos.com; p. I: Jim Young/Reuters/Corbis; p. III:Taylor S. Kennedy/Getty Images; p. IV: Bruce T. Smith/Shutterstock Inc. (top right), digital vision/First Light (top left); p.3: John Sylvester Photography/First Light; p. 4: John Sylvester Photography/First Light; p. 5: John Sylvester/Alamy (bottom); p. 6: Ingram Publishing/MaXx Images; p. 7: A.G.E. Foto Stock/First Light (top), Photoresearchers/First Light (inset); p. 8: Image Bank/Getty Images; p. 9: John Sylvester Photography/First Light; p. 10: Radius Images/Jupiter Images; p. 11: Getty Images; p. 12: Unknown artist, Micmac Indians c. 1850, National Gallery of Canada, Ottawa; p.13: Bettmann/CORBIS (top), Photoresearchers/First Light (bottom); p. 14: Hemis/Alamy; p. 17: Bettmann/CORBIS; p. 19: Library and Archives Canada/C-000733 (top), Barrett & Mackay Photo/All Canada Photo (bottom); p. 20: Public Archives and Records Office of Prince Edward Island, Acc4395/1; p. 21: Dave Bartruff/Corbis (top), Jan Butchofsky-Houser/CORBIS (bottom); p. 22: David Nunuk/First Light; p. 23: Richard Ross/Getty Images; p. 24: Radius Images/First Light; p. 25: Barrett & Mackay ©AllCanadaPhotos.com (bottom), Silvano Audisio/Shutterstock Inc. (top right), Jovan Nikolic/Shutterstock Inc. (top left), Valery Potapova/Shutterstock Inc. (top middle); pp. 26-27: Daryl Benson/Getty Images; pp. 28-29: Watts/Hall Inc/First Light (top); p. 28: John Sylvester ©AllCanadaPhotos.com (bottom); p. 29: Vespasian/Alamy (bottom right), Andrew J. Martinez/Photo Researchers, Inc. (top left), Pennyimages/Shutterstock Inc. (middle left), Teamarbeit/Shutterstock Inc. (bottom left); p. 30: John Sylvester Photography/First Light; p. 31: Barrett & Mackay Photo/All Canada Photo; p. 32: Jean B. Heguy Photo/First Light; p. 33: REUTERS/Mike Cassese (bottom), Valentin Russanov/Shutterstock Inc. (top); p. 34: CP PHOTO/Richard Buchan (top), McCord Museum M114.0-1(inset); p. 35:V. J. Matthew/Shutterstock Inc.; p. 36: Barrett & Mackay ©AllCanadaPhotos.com (top), Maria Bell/Shutterstock Inc. (bottom); p. 37: Jessie Parker/First Light (top), dragon_fang/Shutterstock Inc. (bottom right), Smit/Shutterstock Inc. (bottom left); p. 38: Barrett & Mackay/AllCanadaPhotos.com; p. 39: REUTERS/STRINGER Canada; p. 40:V. J. Matthew/Shutterstock Inc. (top and back cover), Michael Jenner/Alamy (bottom); p. 41: Dave G. Houser/Corbis (bottom), Jan Butchofsky-Houser/CORBIS (top); p. 42: Barrett & Mackay ©AllCanadaPhotos.com (bottom), Library and Archives Canada/C-011299 (top); p. 43: CP PHOTO/Charlottetown Guardian - Nigel Armstrong (top), Monk/Wilmeth Photography/Getty Images (bottom).

Produced by Plan B Book Packagers
Editorial: Ellen Rodger
Design: Rosie Gowsell-Pattison
Special thanks to consultant and editor Terrance Cox, adjunct professor, Brock University, and to Jim Chernishenko.

Library and Archives Canada Cataloguing in Publication

Nielsen, L. Michelle
Prince Edward Island / L. Michelle Nielsen.
(Canada close up)
ISBN 978-0-545-98909-1

1. Prince Edward Island--Juvenile literature. I. Title.
II. Series: Canada close up (Toronto, Ont.)
FC2611.2.N44 2009   j971.7   C2008-906869-6

ISBN-10 0-545-98909-4

6 5 4 3 2 1   Printed in Canada   09 10 11 12 13 14

Contents

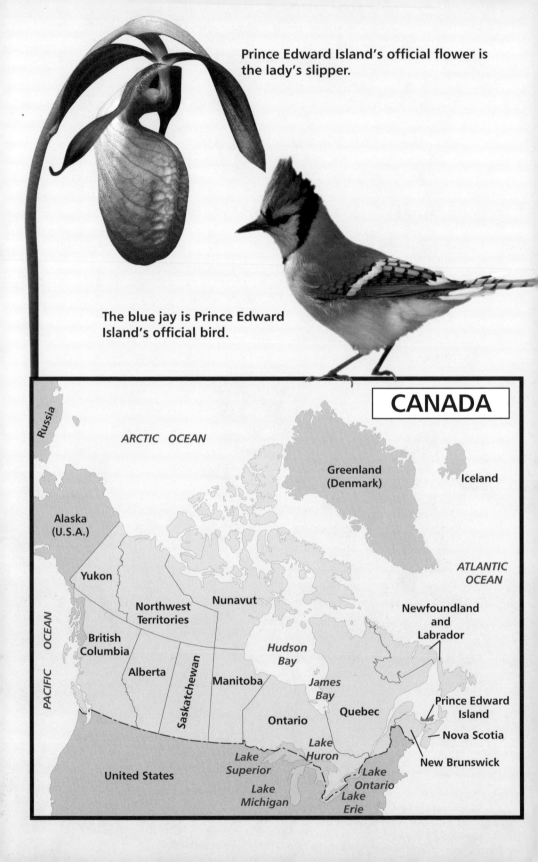

Prince Edward Island's official flower is the lady's slipper.

The blue jay is Prince Edward Island's official bird.

CANADA

Russia

ARCTIC OCEAN

Greenland (Denmark)

Iceland

Alaska (U.S.A.)

Yukon

ATLANTIC OCEAN

PACIFIC OCEAN

Northwest Territories

Nunavut

Newfoundland and Labrador

British Columbia

Hudson Bay

Alberta

Saskatchewan

Manitoba

James Bay

Prince Edward Island

Ontario

Quebec

Nova Scotia

New Brunswick

Lake Huron

Lake Superior

United States

Lake Ontario

Lake Michigan

Lake Erie

Welcome to P.E.I.!

Prince Edward Island is Canada's smallest province in both **area** and population. Though it is only 224 kilometres long and 6 kilometres wide at its narrowest, there are beautiful landscapes at every turn. A drive around the province reveals white sandy beaches, pockets of dense forest, marshy wetlands, green fields and the red soil that the province is famous for.

The real character of the island is created by the nearly 140,000 people who call it home. Many "Islanders," as P.E.I. residents call themselves, put in long, hard hours on farms to make a living. Others may spend their days on the water, harvesting fish and shellfish from the sea. One-third of all Islanders live in the province's only cities – the capital, Charlottetown, and Summerside. But no matter where they live, or what they do, they are proud of being from "the Island."

Chapter 1

Cradled on the Waves

The Mi'kmaq, Prince Edward Island's Aboriginal people, call the island *Epekwitk* (ep-ay-qwi-t-ck). It means "resting on the waves." Around the tiny **crescent** of land ripple the waters of the Gulf of St. Lawrence, making it Canada's only island province.

Mild, wet and breezy

Prince Edward Island receives plenty of rain and is the fourth-snowiest province in Canada. Because it is flat, with no high landforms to stop the winds that come off the ocean, the island's breezes rarely stop blowing. In warmer months it can be battered by the strong winds, heavy rainfall and high tides of a dying Atlantic hurricane. But compared to the two other **Maritime provinces**, P.E.I. has warmer temperatures and fewer days of fog.

In the Gulf of St. Lawrence, cool waters from the Arctic Ocean mix with warmer waters from the Atlantic Ocean and with fresh water from the St. Lawrence River.

Fishing villages occupy the island's many natural harbours and bays.

Not always "the Island"

Prince Edward Island was once connected to the mainland. About 10,000 years ago, the last great **ice age** ended. The large rivers of ice, called glaciers, that had covered North America began to melt. As sea levels rose, the valley that is now the Northumberland Strait flooded, cutting P.E.I. off from the mainland and making it into an island. Today P.E.I. is separated from its mainland neighbours – New Brunswick and Nova Scotia – by the Northumberland Strait.

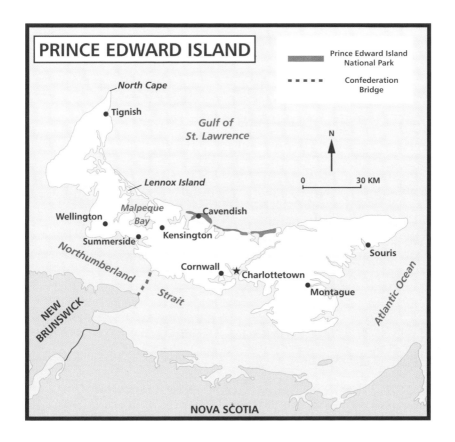

PRINCE EDWARD ISLAND

Prince Edward Island
National Park

Confederation
Bridge

North Cape
Tignish
Gulf of
St. Lawrence
N
0   30 KM
Lennox Island
Malpeque
Bay   Cavendish
Wellington
Summerside   Kensington
Northumberland   Souris
Cornwall
Charlottetown   Atlantic Ocean
Strait   Montague
NEW
BRUNSWICK
NOVA SCOTIA

Prince Edward Island is bursting with colour. Surrounded by the
deep blue ocean, green fields and red soil make up most of the
landscape. In the warmer months, wildflowers paint the island in
shades of yellow, purple, pink, blue and white.

A never-ending coastline

The ice age also helped shape P.E.I.'s ragged coast, resulting in many inlets, bays and harbours. Today the island has 1107 kilometres of coastline. Of that, 800 kilometres is beach. But not all of the beaches look the same. The north shore mostly has sandy beaches. The beaches along the south shore are mostly lined with low, red sandstone cliffs.

Off the northernmost tip of the island, called the North Cape, the waters put on a permanent display. Here the tides of the Northumberland Strait meet the tides of the Gulf of St. Lawrence, creating a visible line in the water.

There's lots of ocean life to discover on a P.E.I. beach!

Great blue herons and many other kinds of birds can be spotted in the wetlands of Prince Edward Island National Park.

Hidden waters

Prince Edward Island is surrounded by lots of water. But it is salt water, and fresh water is what people and animals need to drink. Five per cent of the island is covered in wetlands – marshy, boggy areas soaked in fresh water or salt water. They play an important part in the **water cycle** and provide **habitats** for many plants and animals. Though there are few freshwater lakes and rivers here, the soil easily absorbs water, so rainwater seeps underground and feeds streams that criss-cross the island.

Small villages and farms dot the P.E.I. countryside.

Moving sand dunes

The island's only national park has a special feature: large, moving mounds of sand called **parabolic sand dunes**. Pushed by the winds blowing in off the Gulf, the sand dunes travel two to four metres toward the inland forest each year. As the dunes move, a type of vegetation called marram grass traps some of the sand, forming ridges. Walking on the grass can damage it, so to help **preserve** this rare dune system, it is very important for people to "keep off the grass!"

Prince Edward Island National Park is a long strip of land along the northern coast. Here sand dunes, beautiful beaches, sandstone cliffs, forests and wetlands are home to countless plants and animals.

A red dirt road borders a P.E.I. forest.

New forests

Almost half of Prince Edward Island is covered in forest. Most of the trees are coniferous – with needles instead of leaves. Long ago, the forests were mainly made up of deciduous hardwood trees, like the provincial tree, the red oak. Deciduous trees have leaves that change colour and drop off in the fall. Most of the original forests on the island were cleared by settlers for farmland, or for timber to make ships.

Island info

- P.E.I. is just 5656 square kilometres. (British Columbia's Vancouver Island is nearly six times as large.)

- P.E.I. averages 23 people per square kilometre – more than any other province or territory in Canada.

- Almost half of the island is farmland.

- Confederation Bridge is an engineering marvel. It curves for 12.9 kilometres over the Northumberland Strait to link P.E.I. to New Brunswick. It is the longest bridge designed to span ice-covered waters in the world.

- Many types of whales feed in the Gulf waters around P.E.I.: humpbacks, belugas, minkes and finbacks – even blue whales, the largest creatures on Earth! Near the shore you can see porpoises and seals.

Chapter 2
Looking Back

Before Europeans arrived, Prince Edward Island looked a lot different than it does today. The island was covered in forests and was home to large wild animals such as black bears and caribou. The waters around it were full of fish and other sea life. The only people who lived on the island were the Mi'kmaq.

According to Mi'kmaq beliefs, the Great Spirit created the Earth and all life on it. When he was finished, he had a large clump of red clay left over. He moulded it into a crescent-shaped island, covered it with trees and flowers, and placed it in the Gulf of St. Lawrence. He had made Epekwitk.

P.E.I.'s first European settlers

The first written account of the island was by explorer Jacques Cartier, who landed here in 1534 and declared it "the fairest land that may possibly be seen." In 1603 French explorer Samuel de Champlain claimed the island for France and named it Île Saint-Jean.

Jacques Cartier

But it wasn't until 1720 that the first French settlement was built. Three hundred settlers from France arrived at Port la Joie, across the harbour from what is now Charlottetown. They grew crops to help feed the soldiers stationed at Louisbourg, a major French fort on Cape Breton, in Nova Scotia. The fort was an important defence against the British, who were at war with France in Europe and who also were building settlements in North America.

Samuel de Champlain

The Acadians

French **colonists** lived in what is now New Brunswick and Nova Scotia 100 years before they came to Île Saint-Jean. Their colony was called *L'Acadie*. As Acadia steadily grew, the settlers began to think of themselves not as citizens of France, but as Acadians.

In 1713 the Treaty of Utrecht gave Britain control over parts of Acadia. In 1720 the first Acadian settlers moved to Île Saint-Jean, which remained a French colony, from Nova Scotia. Two thousand more Acadians arrived on the island in 1755, after having escaped the Acadian Expulsion in Nova Scotia. They were **expelled** from Nova Scotia for refusing to be loyal to Britain.

When the French fort of Louisbourg, on Cape Breton, fell to the British in 1758, Île Saint-Jean became a British colony. There were nearly 4500 settlers on the island at that time. Of those, 3100 Acadians were rounded up and shipped to France. Only a few hundred Acadians on the island avoided capture.

The British land lottery

The British took control of the island and chose a site for its capital. They named the capital Charlottetown in honour of Queen Charlotte, the wife of the king of England. The rest of the island was divided into 67 lots of land within three counties.

Supporters of King George III in England were entered in a land lottery. The winning landlords were to send settlers to farm the land. The first of these settlers were the first Scots on P.E.I. They worked hard to clear the land and plant and harvest crops. But they didn't own the land they worked. Instead, they had to pay the landlord a rent. If they fell behind in their rent, they could be kicked off the land.

The landlords, in turn, were required to pay rent to the government for the land they owned. But many of the **absentee landlords** didn't send any settlers or pay any rent, which would have helped support the colony. Instead, they sold and traded the land among themselves in England.

This angered the settlers. They wanted to own the land that they worked, and they pressured the government to act. The government passed a law in 1853 that would allow it to buy the land and sell it to the settlers. Unfortunately, the government did not have much money, and few landlords wanted to sell. In the 1860s the settlers rioted and refused to pay their rent. Prince Edward Island's leaders needed a solution to their land problems. Perhaps the solution would be to join Confederation.

When the Amercian revolution ended in 1783, 6000 Loyalists moved to the island. It was named Prince Edward Island in 1799. This picture shows a Loyalist in the United States being humiliated in public.

Confederation: yes or no?

In the 1860s Canada was made up of separate British colonies. In the Maritimes, Nova Scotia and New Brunswick were thinking of forming one large colony, and they planned to meet with P.E.I. to discuss the possibility of a Maritime Union.

To the west was the Province of Canada – now Ontario and Quebec. It, too, wanted to join into a union. So, on September 1, 1864, representatives from the colonies met in Charlottetown, P.E.I. The union proposed by the Province of Canada turned out to be the first step to Confederation, or the joining of the colonies to make the country of Canada. One of the offers to P.E.I. at the meeting, called the Charlottetown Conference, was money to buy the rest of the land from the landlords. A few weeks later, at a second meeting called the Quebec Conference, the offer was withdrawn. Because of this, P.E.I. decided not to join Canada when it was created on July 1, 1867. Even though P.E.I. did not join at that time, Charlottetown is now known as the "cradle of Confederation."

The representatives at the Charlottetown Conference gather for a photograph.

Discussions took place in this room at Province House, the colony's legislative building.

The little island joins in

At the time of Confederation, Prince Edward Island's economy was strong. Farms were doing so well that there were extra crops to sell to the United States. People on the island had developed their own way of thinking, dressing, eating and speaking. If they became a part of Canada they felt that, as a small province, their voice would not be heard.

Then, in 1873, Canada promised P.E.I. $800,000 to buy the plots of land from the British landlords. The land could then be sold to Islanders, some of whom had farmed there for generations. Canada also offered to pay off the money the colony owed from building its railway. Prince Edward Island accepted the offer and became a province of Canada in 1873.

One of P.E.I.'s first railway trains

Peopling P.E.I.

- Most people in P.E.I. claim English, Scottish and Irish heritage. Many of these people are the **descendants** of the settlers who came in the late 1700s and early 1800s.

- About one per cent of the population of P.E.I. today is Mi'kmaq.

- Descendants of the Acadians who escaped deportation to France still live on the island today. Approximately two per cent of the population is of Acadian descent.

- Islanders refer to anyone not born on the island as a "come-from-away."

Finding its way

There were hard times after Confederation. In the 1800s Islanders had prospered, thanks to a strong shipbuilding industry, but now ships were being built using steel. Ships made from island wood were no longer needed. Many Islanders left P.E.I. for Canada's west or the United States to find jobs.

Things began to look up for the province when motorized tractors and harvesters made farming easier in the 1950s. Farms grew larger and more crops were produced. Tourism also began to develop on the island and more ferries brought visitors from the mainland.

A ferry brings travellers from Nova Scotia to P.E.I.

Chapter 3
Spuds, Seafood and Sightseers

What do most people think of when they think of Prince Edward Island? Potatoes!

Potatoes were first brought to P.E.I. in the late 1760s by Acadians. They were easy to grow and soon became a main source of food. The secret to their success is in the soil. The soil on the island comes from sandstone, and is slightly **acidic** and rich in iron. When the iron is exposed to air, it rusts. This is why the soil is red.

Combine the soil with the climate, and P.E.I. has perfect conditions for growing potatoes, as well as grains, soybeans, berries and vegetables. Many farmers today also raise livestock for beef, pork and dairy products.

More than 30 types of potatoes grow in P.E.I.

From spud to french fry

The humble potato is the top agricultural money-maker on the island. It brings in more money than all other crops put together! The province is known all over the world for its top quality spuds, and it produces between one-third and one-half of all the potatoes grown in Canada each year. Sixty per cent of them are brought to processing plants where they are made into foods such as potato chips and french fries. These plants provide jobs for hundreds of Islanders. P.E.I. has even been given the nickname "Spud Island"!

(right) Roadside stands sell newly grown potatoes.

(left) Potato plants flourish in the island's red soil.

Come play on my island

Tourism brings in a lot of money – enough to make it Prince Edward Island's second most important industry. Visitors from across Canada and all over the globe flock to the island to enjoy its sandy beaches, lobster dinners, golf courses, hiking trails and national and provincial parks.

Thousands of tourists come just to visit the sites written about in *Anne of Green Gables*, a novel set on the island that has been read by millions of people around the world. And thanks to the completion of Confederation Bridge in 1997, visitors can now drive to P.E.I. in just 10 minutes, instead of taking the 75-minute ferry ride from the mainland.

Confederation Bridge created a fixed link to the rest of Canada.

Living off the sea

With so much water all around, it's no wonder that the fishing industry has long been an important part of P.E.I.'s economy. Herring, tuna and salmon are popular catches for fishers, but the most money comes from catching lobster and shellfish such as oysters, clams and mussels. There are also plants that process the seafood by canning it or preparing it for export to other provinces or countries.

Irish moss, a seaweed, is gathered at the island's western shore. It is used in making toothpaste, pie filling, pudding and ice cream.

(above) Fishing boats at Malpeque Harbour

Malpeque Bay on the north coast is world-famous for its tasty oysters. They are grown on the seabed in oyster farms. Fishers harvest them from their boats using long tongs.

Clam

Oysters

Mussels

Fox fur

In the early 1900s clothing made from animal fur was very fashionable. Silver fox fur was sought after all over the world. Prince Edward Island became known for producing large numbers of quality silver fox **pelts**. Instead of hunting wild foxes, Islanders came up with the idea of raising foxes on farms, which gave them a large and reliable source for pelts. The industry boomed on the island for almost forty years. Luckily for the foxes, wearing furs went out of fashion and fox farming died out on the island.

The wind farm at North Cape

A powerful breeze

Prince Edward Island is one of Canada's leaders when it comes to wind research. Wind power is renewable, which means it will never run out. It is also a "clean," or non-polluting, energy source. The North Cape, on the northwest tip of the island, is one of the windiest places in Canada. There, sixteen **wind turbines** generate enough electricity to power over 4000 homes.

Chapter 4
Island Living

Prince Edward Island has just two cities but many small towns and villages. The province's small size gives it the feeling of being one large community. The entire population of the province is less than 140,000 people. This is much smaller than the population of many Canadian cities! If an Islander doesn't know another Islander, they are sure to know someone who is related or is a friend.

The pier at Summerside, the smaller of the island's two cities

Island spirit

Throughout the year, P.E.I. hosts many celebrations. There are agricultural festivals, theatre performances and arts and crafts fairs. The biggest demonstration of the spirit of the island is the Charlottetown Festival. Each year from May to October, people from the island and across Canada come to watch and perform in plays, concerts and musical theatre.

A fiddle is also called a violin.

Many communities on Prince Edward Island were settled by immigrants from Scotland and Ireland. They celebrate their heritage in ceilidhs (kae-leez). A ceilidh is a party at which people tell stories, eat, dance and play **Celtic** music on bagpipes, fiddles and other traditional instruments.

Canadian folk singer Stompin' Tom Connors grew up in P.E.I. One of his most famous songs is "Bud the Spud," about a potato farmer from the island of the "bright red mud."

Tourists treasure souvenirs such as this Mi'kmaq basket made from birchbark and decorated with dyed porcupine quills.

Traditional ways

Many of the artists who live on the island specialize in crafts that have been made since the first settlers arrived. Studios and craft stores sell handmade pottery, baskets, quilts and hooked rugs made from scrap pieces of fabric. Early settlers on the island had to make much of what they needed themselves. Items were expensive and hard to get from the mainland. Today these crafts are a valuable way of keeping P.E.I.'s past alive.

At one time, ships were the only way to transport everything that came to the island — including people, food and other goods. To help ships find the right port, lighthouses were built to guide them. Today there are 55 lighthouses along the shores of P.E.I.

Tasty treats

Potatoes and seafood are **staples** in P.E.I. cooking. Community-wide lobster dinners started as a way of raising money for churches. Everyone who attended brought an item of food, such as coleslaw, homemade rolls, mussels or seafood chowder. The lobsters were cooked and sold by the church. Lobster suppers still take place on the island today as fundraisers.

What do Islanders do with potatoes? Lots! They bake them, or make them into pancakes, scones or soup. They even stuff them with P.E.I. lobster!

Lobster traps

Many Islanders enjoy lobster dinners during the summer, when the shellfish are in season.

Preserves are a favourite treat on the island. Blueberries, cranberries, strawberries and raspberries are some of the main fruits grown here. These are made into jams and jellies.

Chapter 5
The Island's Orphan

On a map of the world, Prince Edward Island is a tiny Canadian jewel. But that tiny treasure is world-famous, thanks in large part to a fictional redhead. In 1908 Islander Lucy Maud Montgomery published a novel about a young orphan named Anne Shirley.

In the story, free-spirited Anne is sent from Nova Scotia to P.E.I. to live with an elderly brother and sister on their farm. Anne soon charms her way into their hearts – and into the hearts of millions of readers. Montgomery went on to write seven more books about Anne's life. They have been translated into more than twenty languages and have sold millions of copies around the world. Anne is especially loved in Japan, and her story brings thousands of Japanese tourists to P.E.I. every year.

Most visitors to the island stop in Cavendish to see Green Gables, the farmhouse that inspired Montgomery's famous novel.

In 2008 Canada Post issued stamps to celebrate the 100th birthday of the novel *Anne of Green Gables*.

Montgomery's P.E.I.

With her writing, L.M. Montgomery showed the world a magical view of her island home. Montgomery adored everything about P.E.I., from its small, shining lakes to the mounding sand dunes and the character of each individual tree. While her many books were intended for children, people of all ages fell in love with them. Of her twenty novels, nineteen were set in P.E.I. Montgomery also wrote hundreds of short stories, poems and hymns, but her most famous work was *Anne of Green Gables*.

An Anne Shirley doll

A bedroom at Green Gables

At Avonlea, fans of *Anne of Green Gables* can tour the storybook village to see what Prince Edward Island was like during L.M. Montgomery's time.

Chapter 6
Points of Pride

▶ In 1943 L.M. Montgomery was made a "person of national historical significance" by the Historic Sites and Monuments Board of Canada. In 2000 *Maclean's* magazine chose L.M. Montgomery as one of 25 Canadians to have "inspired the world."

▶ When you walk along the beach at the eastern end of P.E.I., the sands make a squeaking or whistling sound, which is thought to be due the shape of the sand grains. They have been named the "singing sands."

▶ In 1979 island fisherman Ken Fraser snagged the largest blue fin tuna ever caught. It weighed 679 kilograms.

▶ P.E.I. was the first province to elect a female premier – Catherine Callbeck – in 1993.

▶ In 2007 Robert Ghiz became Canada's youngest-ever premier at age 33.

▶ About 4000 ships were built by hand in P.E.I. during the "golden age of shipbuilding" in the mid to late 1800s.

▶ Lennox Island, off the north shore of P.E.I., is home to the province's largest Aboriginal community.

▶ The city of Summerside is home to the College of Piping and Celtic Performing Arts of Canada, the only full-year piping school in North America. There, students learn to master Celtic instruments, such as the bagpipes, and highland dancing.

Glossary

absentee landlords: Owners of land who live elsewhere

acidic soil: Soil in which most minerals and nutrients are soluble or available

area: The extent of a surface

Celtic: Describes the language and culture of the Celts, a group of western European peoples

colonists: People who leave their country to settle in a new land

crescent: A half-moon shape

descendants: People whose background can be traced to a certain group or person

expelled: Forced to leave

ice age: A period in history when most of Earth was covered in ice

habitats: The natural areas where animals live

Loyalists: Colonists who supported Britain during the American Revolution

Maritime provinces: New Brunswick, Nova Scotia and Prince Edward Island. Maritime means "near the sea."

parabolic sand dunes: Sand dunes that form when vegetation holds part of them in place and steady winds push the rest forward

pelts: The skins of fur-bearing mammals with the hair still on

preserve: Keep undisturbed

staples: Basic or main ingredients

water cycle: The constant movement of Earth's water, from Earth's surface to the air and back to Earth

wind turbines: Engines that use propellers and energy from the wind to make electricity